The Last Supper
and Other Bible Favorites

ARCTURUS

The Last Supper

Mark 14:25 "I tell you, I will never again drink this wine until the day I drink the new wine in the Kingdom of God."

At the end of the Passover celebrations, it was time for the Passover meal. Jesus knew that his enemies were looking for him, so the Passover meal to be shared with his friends would have to be held in secret. The disciples asked where Jesus wanted to have the meal, as Jerusalem was overcrowded. But many people were happy to share their homes with Jesus and he had already made arrangements for the meal that evening.

In reply to his disciples, Jesus said, "Go to the city and find a man carrying a jar of water. He will lead you to a house. Ask the owner of the house to show you the room upstairs where you can prepare the meal and we will eat there."

The disciples soon found the man carrying the water, as usually only women carried water. Everything happened as Jesus had told them and they

prepared their meal in the upstairs room of the house.

That evening, Jesus and his disciples sat down to eat. In those days, the least important servant washed the feet of guests who had walked along dusty roads. A jug of water and towel lay ready, but no servants were present and not one of the disciples was prepared to do such a lowly job.

Jesus poured some water into a basin and picked up the towel. Then he knelt before each disciple and washed their feet.

When Jesus had finished his task, he said, "You see? I am prepared to do anything for you. You must be ready too, to serve each other. Don't always think of yourselves and your own importance."

Later, as they sat at the table eating, drinking, and talking, Jesus looked around, smiled sadly, and said, "One of you will betray me to my enemies."

The disciples were horrified. "You can't mean me?" asked each one.

When one of the disciples, Judas Iscariot, asked this, Jesus replied, "Yes, you are the one."

Then he broke a piece of bread and shared it with everyone. "This is my body," he said. "When you break and eat bread together like this, remember me."

Then Jesus passed a cup of wine among them. "Drink this, all of you," he said. "This is my blood, which will be poured out so that everyone's sins can be forgiven by God."

Did you know?

Today, people celebrate Passover by eating "matzo," a flat bread similar to the bread the Israelites ate after their departure from Egypt.

The Garden of Gethsemane

Luke 22:48 Jesus said, "Judas, is it with a kiss that you betray the Son of Man?"

Jesus and the disciples finished the Passover meal and then went for a walk to a quiet place outside the city.

"You will all run away from me," Jesus told them.

"Never!" exclaimed Peter. "I'd die with you if necessary."

The others all agreed.

Jesus shook his head. "Peter," he said, "before the cock crows tomorrow, three times you will have said that you don't know me."

"Never!" repeated Peter.

Jesus and his disciples reached a garden called Gethsemane.

Gathering his disciples, Jesus said, "Wait here while I pray. I am very sad. Please keep watch for me."

Walking a short distance away from the others, Jesus threw himself on the ground. "Please, Father!" he prayed, "don't let me suffer!"

Jesus prayed once more and spoke again, this time more calmly, "Don't do what I want, but do what you know is best."

Some time later, Jesus returned to his friends, who had fallen asleep. "Couldn't you have stayed awake just for one more hour?" he asked, disappointed. "Now you will have to wake up, because I'm going to be taken prisoner. Look! Here comes the one who has betrayed me."

A rough-looking crowd, including temple guards armed with sticks and spears, was walking toward them. At the front of the crowd was Judas Iscariot.

"The man I kiss is the one you want," he whispered to the guards, and walked boldly up to Jesus.

"Hello, Teacher," Judas said, and kissed Jesus on the cheek.

Jesus looked at Judas. "My friend," he said sadly, "are you betraying me with a kiss?"

Peter was furious as the guards rushed forward and seized Jesus. Pulling out a sword, Peter lashed out wildly, cutting a guard's ear.

"Put your sword away, Peter!" said Jesus. "If I wished to go free, I could call armies of angels to fight for me. But I am ready to give up my life according to God's plan."

Gently, Jesus reached out and touched the guard's bleeding ear, which healed instantly. Then he said to his captors, "Why are you treating me like a criminal? Every day I sat teaching in the temple, but you didn't arrest me then." The men did not answer.

Jesus knew that the priests who had him arrested were afraid of his crowd of followers. But as Jesus was taken out of the garden, his terrified disciples ran away.

Did you know?

The garden of Gethsemane is at the foot of the Mount of Olives in Jerusalem.

Peter Denies Jesus

Luke 22:56-57 She said: "This man was with him too,"
but he denied it, saying, "Woman, I do not know him."

The guards took Jesus to the house of Caiaphas, the high priest. It was still evening, but the priests had decided they must put Jesus on trial at once to avoid trouble from his followers.

Meanwhile, Peter and another disciple had stopped running. They suddenly realized how cowardly they were being and decided to follow the guards to see where Jesus was being taken.

When Peter and his companion reached the house of Caiaphas, they asked a servant girl at the gate if they could go in. "Yes," she answered, then looked closely at Peter. "Aren't you a disciple of that man?" she asked, pointing toward a room where Jesus had been taken.

"No, I am not!" replied Peter, afraid that he might be arrested for cutting the guard's ear. He shivered and made his way to warm his hands at the hot coal fire in the courtyard. A man standing nearby stared at Peter. "Aren't you one of that man's disciples?" he asked.

Afraid of what might happen to him the conversation was overheard, Peter bowed his head and replied, "No, I am not!"

In the corner of the courtyard, some servants were discussing the latest events. They looked across at Peter and one called out, "You are one of the prisoner's friends. You can't deny it, I saw you with him— and you come from Galilee, too. You have the same accent!"

Everyone stared at Peter, who lost his temper. "I tell you, I don't know who you're talking about," he shouted angrily.

Just then, dawn began to light up the dark sky and somewhere a cock crowed. Peter remembered what Jesus had said to him a few hours earlier: "Before the cock crows tomorrow, three times you will have said that you don't know me."

Ashamed, Peter looked through the window to where Jesus was standing, being questioned by his enemies. Jesus looked back at him kindly. Peter felt terrible. He had failed someone who had never let him down. He rushed out of the courtyard, crying bitterly.

Did you know?

Peter is one of the most important of Jesus' twelve disciples, and Jesus calls him his "rock." He was the first to call Jesus "the Messiah," which means "anointed by God."

The Trial of Jesus

Mark 15:9-10 "Do you want me to set free for you the king of the Jews?" He knew very well that the chief priests had handed Jesus over to him because they were jealous.

Jesus was blindfolded and beaten and put on trial before the Council of Jewish leaders. The council tried hard to prove his guilt, but none of the witnesses told the same story. Then the high priest, Caiaphas, demanded of Jesus, "Are you the Son of God?"

"I am," replied Jesus.

"Ha!" answered Caiaphas. "We don't need any more witnesses. He has said he is like a god, and for this he deserves to die."

Only the Romans were allowed to put people to death, so Jesus was sent to the Roman governor, Pontius Pilate. "This troublemaker tells people not to pay taxes and says he is their king," the priests told him.

If this was true, Jesus could be sentenced to death, but Pilate was sure the religious leaders had made up the charges because they were jealous of Jesus.

"Are you the king of the Jews?" Pilate asked. But Jesus would answer no more questions.

Pilate was sure Jesus was innocent, but outside his palace the priests were stirring up trouble and people were chanting, "Crucify him!" Pilate had an idea.

"It's Passover," he called to the mob. "As part of the celebrations, I always set one prisoner free. This man has done nothing to deserve death, so shall he be set free?"

"No!" yelled the crowd. "Free Barabbas, instead!" Barabbas was in prison for murder. Pilate shrugged and ordered his soldiers to set Barabbas free.

Meanwhile, other soldiers beat Jesus and forced a crown of thorny twigs onto his head. They wrapped a purple cloak around him, and jeered, "Long live the King!"

At last, Pilate took Jesus out to the crowd. The same people who had welcomed Jesus into Jerusalem only five days before now roared, "Let him die on the cross!"

Did you know?

Crucifixion was meant to shame those being executed and to warn onlookers not to do what they had done.

The Crucifixion

Mark 15:39 And the curtain of the temple was torn in two from top to bottom. And when the centurion who was standing opposite him saw how he died, he said, "Truly this man was a son of God."

Jesus was led away to die. Under Jewish law, he had to be killed outside the city gates. The Roman soldiers made him carry the heavy wooden cross to a place called Golgotha. A mocking crowd followed and Jesus, weak from being questioned and beaten, stumbled beneath the weight of the cross.

A broad-shouldered man called Simon was there, who had come from North Africa for Passover,

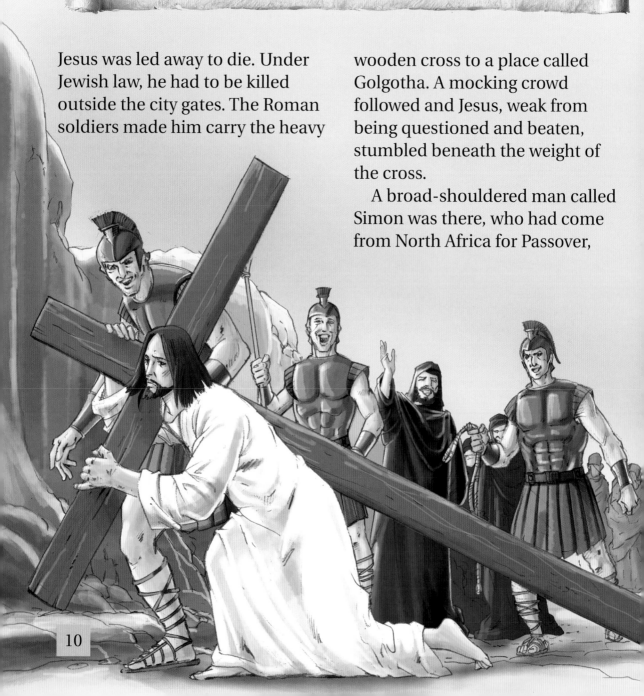

and the soldiers grabbed him. "Carry the cross for the prisoner," they called, "or we'll never get there." Simon helped Jesus for the rest of the way to Golgotha. Then the words "The King of the Jews" were written on the cross.

When they reached the hill, the soldiers laid Jesus down on the cross and hammered nails through his feet and wrists. Jesus said, "Father, forgive them, for they do not realize what they are doing."

Two robbers were put on crosses on either side of him. The crosses were set into the ground and lifted up, so that the men would die from heat and thirst. It was nine o'clock in the morning, so the soldiers sat down and began gambling with dice to pass the time until the prisoners died.

When the religious leaders arrived, they taunted, "You saved others, but you can't save yourself."

Then one of the two robbers called out, "Aren't you the Chosen One? Save yourself and us!"

"Don't say that," interrupted the other robber. "We are both getting what we deserve, but this man has done nothing wrong!" Then turning toward Jesus, he said, "Remember me when you reach your kingdom."

"Today you will be with me in Paradise," replied Jesus.

Some of Jesus' friends were there, crying. Jesus whispered down to John, "Look after my mother and be a son to her."

At midday, when the sun should have been at its brightest, the sky turned black and Jesus called out, "My God, why have you deserted me?" By three o'clock, he gasped, "I'm so thirsty!"

A soldier soaked a sponge in sour wine and held it up to moisten Jesus' dry lips. Then in a clear voice, Jesus said, "It's finished!"

At that moment, back in Jerusalem, the curtain in the temple was torn in two. At Golgotha, Jesus bowed his head and died.

Did you know?

The name Christ comes from the Greek word "Christos." Like "Messiah," it means "anointed" or "chosen one."

Jesus Rises
from the Grave

Mark 16:10-11 She went and told his companions. They were mourning and crying, and when they heard her say that Jesus was alive and that she had seen him, they did not believe her.

Pontius Pilate agreed that two of Jesus' followers could give him a proper burial. They took his body, wrapped it in strips of cloth, and took it to a garden where a new grave had been cut into a rock. The Pharisees were worried that the disciples would steal the body and pretend that Jesus had risen, so they sealed the tomb and Roman soldiers stood guard over it.

Some of the women who had been Jesus' friends watched the burial. Worn out with sadness and crying, they left. It was Friday evening and the next day was the Sabbath, the Jewish day of rest. They could do nothing but mourn and wait for the day to pass.

As soon as Saturday evening came, the women began preparing perfumes and spices to put on Jesus' body. They wanted to show how much they cared for him.

Early on Sunday morning, Mary Magdalene and some of the other women, made their way to the garden. When they arrived, the guards had gone and the huge rock sealing the grave had been moved aside, leaving the tomb wide open. Mary Magdalene ran to get Peter and John. They peered inside the cave. On the floor lay the grave cloths and Jesus' body had gone. Peter and John went back to the other disciples but Mary remained, tears pouring down her cheeks. She looked into the tomb again and saw two angels, sitting where Jesus' body had been.

"Why are you crying?" asked a man's voice. She had not noticed anyone else in the garden and supposed he was the gardener. "Sir," she replied, "they have moved Jesus' body. Do you know where it is?"

"Mary!" exclaimed the man, and suddenly she recognized him. It was Jesus.

"Master!" she cried.

"Go and tell my disciples that I have risen and am on my way to our Father," said Jesus, smiling.

Mary ran out of the garden, her sadness lifted. She burst in on the grieving group of disciples and cried, "He's alive! He's really alive!"

Did you know?

The Jewish Sabbath is from sunset on Friday to sunset on Saturday. It recalls the creation of the world by God in six days, while on the seventh He rested.

The Ascension

Acts 1:11 *"This Jesus, who has been taken away from you up to Heaven, will come in the same way as you have seen him go."*

For forty days, Jesus appeared to his friends at different times. He looked and seemed different, but there was no doubt that he was alive. He ate meals with the disciples and talked with them as he had done before he was crucified. But now he could pass through closed doors and appear or disappear at will. He helped the disciples to understand a lot more about the scriptures than they had before.

On the fortieth day after he had risen in the garden, he walked with them to the Mount of Olives and

turned to them. "You must tell everyone all about what has happened," he said. "Go and preach the Gospel everywhere, and make your own disciples, baptizing them in the name of the Father, the Son, and the Holy Spirit. Once people understand why I suffered and died, then rose again, they will live better lives."

Jesus held up his hands to bless them and spoke once more. "Remember that I will be with you always, just as I always told you."

Did you know?

The Feast of the Ascension is the day that Christians commemorate the rising of Jesus to Heaven. It is usually celebrated on the fortieth day after Easter Sunday.

Then he rose up into the sky and disappeared behind a cloud. The disciples returned to Jerusalem and went to the temple every day to thank God for Jesus.

One morning, six weeks later, Jerusalem was once more packed with pilgrims, as they had all come to celebrate the festival of Pentecost, the harvest thanksgiving for the first ripe crops.

Something strange happened. The disciples were in a house, when a great rushing wind suddenly blew through the rooms. Then, just for an instant, a small tongue of flame settled on every disciple. Warmth surged through them and they realized that this was the Holy Spirit, sent to them from Heaven.

A large crowd had gathered outside the house. The people had seen and heard the wind and wondered what was happening. The disciples stepped outside, feeling happy for the first time in weeks. But what happened then was even more amazing. Everyone in the street, no matter what country they had come from, understood perfectly what the disciples were saying.

This edition published in 2012 by Arcturus Publishing Limited
26/27 Bickels Yard, 151–153 Bermondsey Street,
London SE1 3HA
Copyright © 2012 Arcturus Publishing Limited
All rights reserved.

ISBN: 978-1-84858-677-2
CH002340US
Supplier 15, Date 0412, Print run 1752

Printed in China